MOU

THE MANIC MOGGIE

Also by Michael O'Hanlon

Free Spirits

MOUSER:

THE MANIC MOGGIE

by

Michael O'Hanlon

Illustrated by the author

2009

Mouser:
The Manic Moggie

First published in 2009
by
Fever Cabin
98 Derrytresk Road
Derrynaheskella
Coalisland
Co. Tyrone
N. Ireland
BT71 4QL

A CIP record for this book
is available from the British Library

ISBN-10 09550720-1-8
ISBN-13 978-0-9550720-1-7

Typesetting and cover design by
Fever Cabin

Printed in Northern Ireland by
Edenderry Print, Belfast

For my family

Special thanks to Bernadette, Aidan and Malachy for posing as Lady LaMond, Sarge and the circus strongman. You filled their stockings, boots and shoes so well.

Thanks also to Oonagh Given for crossing my path with a black cat.

CONTENTS

BEWARE OF THE CAT

About this house you should watch your back,
Her eyes are green and her pelt is black,
She'll coil, then spring like a jumping jack;

If I were you I'd scarper!

Her sight is sharper than a sniper's,
Her fangs more fearsome than a viper's –
Is it any wonder I wear diapers

Instead of underwear?

She runs up the curtains and she jumps on the chairs,
She spins 'round the table and she bounds up the stairs,
She tears up my jeans and she pees in my hair;

My heart is bound to break.

The floorboards shake with her hunger pangs,
I quake in my boots when I see her fangs,
And run to the shops like a boomerang;

Sausages, bacon and chops.

She likes a brew, but have no doubt,
She's like a shrew or a lager lout
When she sets her pout on a pint o' stout,

Or a thimble full of moonshine.

A drop o' wine or a shandy beer,
And, *goodness gracious me man dear!*
She'll swing like a goon from the chandelier

And pee all over the room.

Even if your feet have a mighty stench
Like a pair of kippers or a stinky tench,
She'll clamp on like a monkey wrench

And trim your nails bejapers!

There's a vapour rising off her poo
Which sticks to things like superglue.
Take my advice and wear your shoes,

(Though it's great for catchin' mice).

I'm the goof who pays the rent,
But to tell the truth, I'd be more content,
From time to time, to pitch a tent

In the deepest darkest jungle.

She's the guest, I'm the host,
But she treats my shin like a scratchin' post;
Now my scabby skin's like a piece o' toast

And I'm yappin' like a babby.

'BEWARE OF THE MUTT' on a front doormat
Would be sure to scare the toughest brat,
But when folk see: 'BEWARE OF THE CAT',

They think it's all a joke.

But not the postie; he learned to dread her,
Especially if I hadn't fed her;
'It's like feeding mail through a paper shredder;

I have to wear a gauntlet.'

Our milkman's haunted to this day still;
When he first saw her, his blood was chilled
As white as the milk that ran down the hill

When he crashed and lost his payload.

Along the road the shards were scattered,
So when he reversed, his tyres were tattered
And all the while his dentures chattered,

Like a pair of castanets.

More of a pest and less of a pet,
We took her along to see a vet,
But even he broke out in a sweat

And took on a ghastly look.

But he took a sample, ran a test,
While his face grew even more distressed;
Then said, 'No wonder that cat's a pest!

Brace yourself, by thunder!

The world is seldom what it seems;
But never in my wildest dreams,
Have I seen a moggie with *panther* genes;

Where in Hell did she come from?'

'Where she came from, we'll never know;
She appeared one night 6 months ago
When the steps lay under tiers of snow,

Like a frosty layered cake.'

ON THE PROWL

Any night I'll take your bet,
If the moon is full, her silhouette,
Will sit on the post like a statuette,

Quiet as a ghost.

Just like horse ears twitch an' bevel,
The ears on *her* head pitch an' swivel;
Against the moon, they're like horns on a 'divil';

Turn back and whistle a tune.

She's Dr. Jekyll all day long,
But when the scent of her prey is strong,
She's Mr. Hyde with death bells on;

So put a good spring in your stride.

When she's caterwaulin' like a banshee whingein'
Or the war cry of a Comanche Injin;
There's ringin' in my lugs and I can't stop cringin',

Even with my earplugs.

Through witching hours when wolf packs howl,
Make no mistake, she's on the prowl
And by breakfast time, I'll find an owl,

Stretched out on the welcome mat.

Either that, or a neighbour's dog,
A fluffy sheep or a wild boar hog,
And once in a while, a big bullfrog

Is subject to her guile.

She's not what you'd call a fussy cat,
If she can't have trout, then a fuzzy bat
Will taste as good as a juicy rat,

And she doesn't need a saucepan.

Now I'm not a man given to gamblin',
But if you've more mice than the town of Hamelin,
Then she's the one to sort the handlin' –

Your 1st and last resort.

She'd flush the sewers and never stall,
Strike the alleys like a bowlin' ball
And rush them up in a mighty squall;

Like leaves before a yard-brush.

The ancient Romans ate dormice,
But if I served them up with curry an' rice,
Would you take a nibble at any price

Or pinch your nose and quibble?

Some folk like their meat to be rare,
But she'll eat hers wrapped up in fur,
So if you wear a fur coat, then *you* should beware,

You could be on the menu.

THE SIX STAR PET HOTEL

In need of a break, we made our plans,
And the pet hotel took her off our hands,
But I briefed the owner, Mr. Farlands,

On points he'd have to heed:

'On the hand that feeds she'll clamp her jaw,
For she's red in tooth and red in claw
And it never seems to stick in her craw;

So never chance your arm.

She has her charm but if she's in the mood,
She could nail herself to a piece of wood,
But the neck or face is just as good;

I often wear a neck-brace.

Never ever pull her tail,
You might never live to tell the tale,
Her claws unsheathe, her limbs will flail;

It could only end in grief.

Though her snap would spook an alligator,
When she's had enough food to finally sate her,
She'll purr just like a refrigerator,

Stuffed with grub aplenty.'

He spoke like a gent with a southern drawl:
'I think you'll find we're on the ball,
And we love all creatures, great and small;

In cat care we're the best.

Every guest is so well pampered,
That even a beastly lion or leopard,
Would at least be 10 times better tempered

When they go back home to y'all.

This is what I'd call a 6 starred hotel,
Cos the extra star is Gerard Durrell
Who treats anything feathered or furred, so well,

They think of him as family.'

The cattery certainly had quite a team,
So by Saturday we were living the dream,
Charging our batteries and licking ice cream,

On a beach of golden sand.

All was grand, life was swell,
Till we got a call from Gerry Durrell:
'Come an' take this beast back to Hell,

And get here on the double!

As soon as I saw her, I knew she'd be trouble,
For she nuzzled the air like a hog huntin' truffles,
And only this mornin' she ate three gerbils,

Before she disappeared

Then sheared a sheep, piranha-style,
While the farmer shrieked and ran a mile,
(Though she left the wool in a neat wee pile;

Like an Aussie farmer).

She made for his barn where she ate her fill;
The farmer's arrived just now with the bill;
A chicken, a goat, a sow and her swill;

Nothin' will stick in her throat!'

★ ★ ★ ★ ★ ★

THE COUNTY FAIR

When the money runs out my flesh'll creep
Cos when it comes to grub she'll relish a heap,
We knew she'd have to earn her keep,

So I got my brain cells janglin' –

By danglin' a piece of meat in the air,
We trained her to dance like a dancing bear,
Then took her along to the County Fair:

50 pence to see her.

When I took her around for a walk on the leash
We saw a piglet covered in grease,
Being chased by men in dungarees;

So her ears stood up like flint.

The owner made a mint as dope after dope,
Took it for a breeze, but they hadn't a hope,
For the tighter you squeeze, like a bar a soap;

The faster pigs will fly.

The squeal of the pig and the pong of its pork
Made her claws unsheathe like the prongs of a fork,
And she slipped from my grip like a champagne cork,

As greasy as the pig.

She cleared the fence with a simple bound
An' chased the pig around and 'round,
Just like a hare gets chased by a hound;

So the folks all placed their bets.

The games and rides were all forsaken,
And the odds were good and no mistakin';
It was 5 to 1 she'd take home the bacon.

Easy money for the shrewd.

Then a crazy dude jumped in to bait her,
And swaggered around like a gladiator,
Till she bit him on the rump like an alligator,

And he jumped as high as a kite.

As she closed in tight on the greasy hog,
The punters' eyes were all agog,
And one, no joking, like a big bullfrog,

Went hoarse and started croaking.

The atmosphere began to change,
When she caught the pig and the squeals grew strange
And summoned a man from the rifle-range.

The spectators now were stunned.

An Italian man called Luciano
Appeared with his gun and plenty of ammo.
In a cloud of smoke the gun cried 'BLAMMO!'

And scattered the crowd of folk.

But the clever ruse didn't work,
And Luciano looked like a bungling berk
Cos a noise like that made her go berserk

And she jumped right into the crowd.

A daredevil biker sped past – *varoom!*
Waving a burger like a silly goon,
He threw it in the basket of the big balloon,

Then plunged straight into the pond.

Fond of a snack, she leaped into the basket,
While the rope was cut with a blow from a hatchet.
They were safe for now but they'd have to catch it,

Though you'd sooner catch a pig.

The balloon was as big as a marquee tent,
And on the side was a picture of an elephant,
Yet it took to the air so elegant,

All we could do was stare.

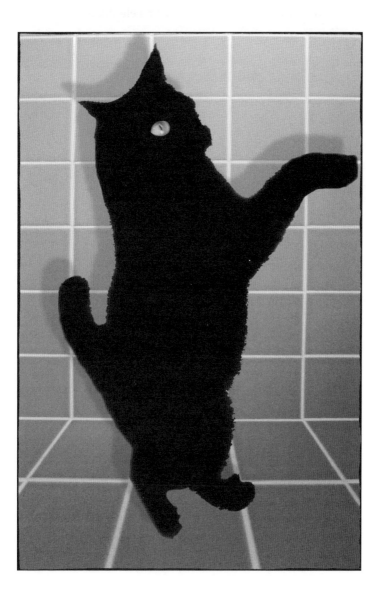

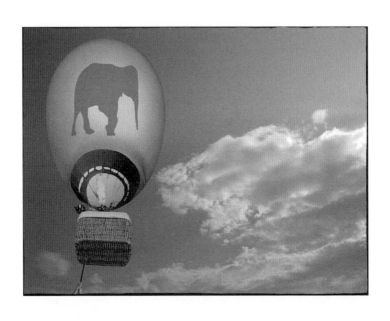

PHILEAS MOGG

As the great balloon lifted into the ether
The balloon man ran like hell for leather,
And with a leap and a bound he grabbed the tether

To keep it on the ground.

But the man had clearly lost his head,
For even if his boots were made of lead,
He'd still be danglin' at the end of the thread,

Like a spider from a ceiling.

Like Tarzan climbing a jungle vine,
At the ripe old age of a hundred and nine,
You could hear him puff, you could hear him whine,

As he fixed his sight on the basket.

The man was as fit as a double bass,
And half way up, with a purple face,
He soldiered on at a woeful pace,

Till he reached his goal then tried

To climb inside but he must've been dumb,
If he thought she'd share the space like a chum,
For she ripped the seat of his pants off his bum,

As he scrambled back onto the rope.

He hadn't a hope, it was plain to see,
But the kids on the ground were choking with glee,
While a number of ladies spat out their tea

As well as their cucumber sarnies.

Put yourself in his trousers and all too soon,
You'll see it's not so funny hangin' from a balloon
With your bum stickin' out like a great baboon;

On a dare you'd chicken out.

With my head in my hands, there seemed no hope,
I didn't know how the hell we'd cope,
Then someone appeared with a telescope

And across our sights they careered.

His grip on the rope grew weak and feeble
As they lost some height and he grabbed a steeple.
You could see his relief, till he saw the people

Pointing from the graveyard.

A crowd had gathered with the parish priest
To bury a man recently deceased,
Then a woman cried out: 'Ya dirty beast!

Come down and show respect.'

The gulls pecked him from his head to his shoes,
As a chopper circled with a TV crew
And filmed it all for the Tea Time News,

Before they got him down.

On the edge of the town she hit a thermal vent
And like an elevator, made her ascent;
Into the skies and away she went,

On her merry way.

There's truly nothin' that a cat must fear
So when she drifted high in the atmosphere,
It was me who sat an' burst in tears,

Like a blubber-puss.

Would our puss go off to Mars
And never again come down from the stars?
Would she meet her fate in meteor showers

Or be the first mog on the moon?

The balloon caught the wind just like a sail
And it swam across the sky just like a whale,
Over meadow, hill and dale

Swept the ghostly sheet of its shadow.

Off she went, away on her flight,
Crossing the sky as high as a kite,

Eyes surveying the whole of the nation:
A fire engine gleaming outside the station,

Houses clustered in housing estates,
Workmen queuing at factory gates,

A river's meander from mountain to coast,
'Tween stubbly fields like pieces of toast,

Scavenging birds on the city dump,
Vehicles queuing at petrol pumps,

Fields ploughed up like corduroy drills,
With hundreds of birds all sinking their bills,

Railtrack stitching the land together;
Pasture, barley, wheat and heather,

A reservoir, as bright as silver,
Reflecting the sun, all a-glimmer,

Ducks at the pond, planes at the airport,
Trucks at the docks, all ready for export,

Boats on the lough, fishing for eels,
A combine harvester shaving the fields,

Kids on their bikes, trees in the woods,
A flea market selling all manner of goods.

Telegraph poles, giant pylons,
Greenhouses glinting just like diamonds,

A-roads, B-roads, rutted lanes,
Pumping the traffic along their veins,

Slated roofs and chimney pots,
Pointed steeples, cemetery plots,

Washing lines and privet hedges,
Potted plants on window ledges...

* * *

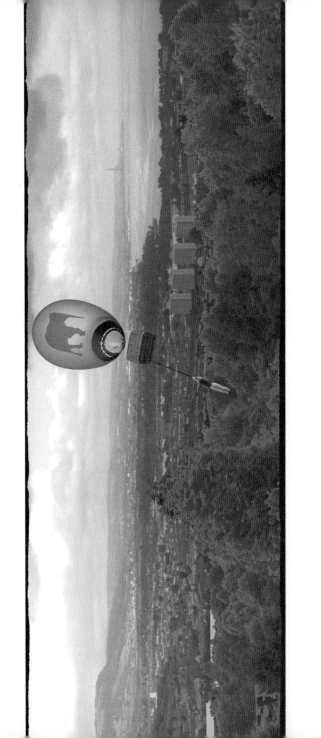

She sailed through the air like Phileas Fogg,
Till the cloud turned dark as Victorian smog,
Then seemed to sink like a cow in a bog,

Or a submarine in the drink.

Thunder and lightning cracked and boomed
And with every flash, the black clouds bloomed.
In that wicker nest, our baby was doomed,

At Mother Nature's breast.

A frightening jolt gave us such a scare,
As a lightning bolt left a great big tear
And she hurtled to the ground like Lucifer,

Cast out of the heavenly realm.

I was overwhelmed by the noise and the bustle,
And when I thought my heart was bound to frazzle,
It seemed she landed on a bouncy castle

Almost as though she planned it!

The 'bouncy castle', truth be told,
Was a circus tent, bright and bold,
Sittin' like a giant jelly-mould,

On the far side of the mount.

*   *   *

Out for the count on the back of a cart
Behind bars of steel, finely wrought,
I could see the tranquillizer dart,

So at least they didn't maim her.

The lion tamer, pleased as punch,
Had this to say over lunch;
'I bet I could tame her when it comes to the crunch,'

So I told him he hadn't a clue:

'If I were *you* I'd clock a mile
If she fixes you with a reptile eye,
For her snap is worse than a crocodile;

There'd be no call for a nurse.

If you pull her tail, be very afraid,
No one's gonna rush to your aid;
It's like pullin' the pin on a hand-grenade;

There's no way to defuse her.'

'Oh she'll obey, and lose her quirks,
For I know how a cat's mind works,
And I'll salt the badness that always lurks,

Behind a wild cat's eyes.'

'She'll read your mind like she'll smell a rat,
She can spin through the air like an acrobat
An' stick to your neck like a velcro-bat:

And then you'll hit the deck.'

'Ah, but I'm the best in the game,
And I'll do more than simply tame;
She'll be jumpin' through the hoops of flame

A week from now, on cue.'

'You can train a mutt to be sweet and civil,
But you're talkin' rot, you're talkin' drivel;
You can't have a pet Tasmanian devil –

But hell, I'll take your bet.'

CHAOS AT THE CIRCUS

They started the show with a big black box
Wrapped up with chains and big padlocks,
Then rolling drums, dry-ice, then shock

When the lock was suddenly sprung.

The lid swung open on the big black box
And with teeth as sharp as any croc's,
Mouser sprang out like a flying fox

As a cymbal crash rang out.

The big cat tamer curled his lip,
Spat out commands, unfurled his whip,
But when it cracked, where was the tip?

In the steely grip of her gnashers.

He tried to lash her, the silly sod,
But she thought the whip was a fishing rod
And rose for the bait like a jumbo cod;

Her timing's never late.

She'll never answer to human laws;
In her own beady mind she has no flaws –
He licks his wounds, she licks her paws;

No man alive could challenge her.

The manager thought he'd have to be sacked,
But night after night the big top was packed,
For the folks still thought it was a comedy act;

And then they topped the bill.

Every night their sides were sore,
Laughing away at their tug-of-war
As the tamer's body ploughed the floor.

She made him bite the sawdust.

Night after night he thought he'd choke
On the gobfulls of sawdust rammed down his throat.
He screamed one night, 'It's beyond a joke,

That's it, I'm gettin' out!'

She was leapin' about like a kangaroo
When the famous old gnarly buckaroo
Who goes by the name of Dan McGrew

Threw his hat into the ring.

When our cat heard the '*ching*' of his spurs,
She licked her chops and whiskers
And just when he should've been singing his prayers,

He cussed and kicked the sawdust.

He picked up the hat and adjusted the brim.
The scene just couldn't look more grim
As he cast out a shadow that was long and slim,

Like a gallows frame at dawn.

Blood would be drawn, an' no mistake.
She crouched down low and hissed like a snake;
Like a duel at dawn, there could be a wake

Before a count of ten.

Then there seemed a change in tempo;
Time slowed down, they were stuck in limbo,
And him with his arms and legs akimbo –

But he never reached his gun.

Before one bead of sweat appeared,
Before he even felt 'afeard',
She was pinned to his jowls like a big black beard;

I've never heard such howls!

The circus strong man grabbed her tail,
And that's when we heard her mighty wail
Sweep and swell like a 10 force gale

And fan the flames of Hell.

The band was scared as stiff as starch,
But they tried their hand at a circus march
In a crass attempt to cover the farce

With blasts of bumbling brass.

Torn from the cheeks of the old gunslinger,
What could the strongman do, but swing her
Like a ball and chain, then finally fling her

Out of the sawdust ring?

Throughout this scene the crowd were rapt till,
She landed among them and they spread like shrapnel,
Screaming and swearing at the top of their lungs till,

Their fortune changed with a pairing –

The Brothers Zamyanoff sprang into action;
They called her name to create a distraction,
But what happened next only heightened the tension,

And we stared with baited breath.

Defying death with skilful ease,
Those daring young men on the flying trapeze
Showed no sign of panic as they swung by their knees,

While Mouser was clearly manic.

She climbed the ladder, then along the high wire,
(The temptation had her driven absolutely haywire),
Her senses were sharp, the outlook dire –

My nerves were strung like a harp.

Her instincts drove her like a machine,
But with every swipe, they got away clean,
Till one of them fell to the trampoline,

And got a close shave as he passed her.

The ringmaster told the crowd not to fret,
While into the ring stepped the circus vet.
With his loaded gun the scene was set

To take another turn.

Shot in the side, she lost her balance,
And found herself hangin' by the tips of her talons.
She'd lost her shine in the deathly silence,

Pegged-out like a rag on a line.

The whole thing seemed so uncivilized –
Hangin' up there so traumatized,
Even if she'd only been tranquillized

Above a safety net.

The circus vet made sure of his luck
Cos he knew he couldn't pass the buck.
He took aim once more at our 'sitting duck'

And again the gun banged

As the tightrope twanged like a double bass string
And she fell like a star to the circus ring.

BIG CATS AT LARGE

We knew there was only one thing to do,
So as not to end up in courtroom stew,
So we signed her over to the City Zoo,

In the hope that they would mind her.

Living next door to Smoky the sealion,
She shared a pen with another feline,
Though he was a bit more 'masculine',

Strutting around their patch.

They were quite a match, like king and queen,
And their pelts were better than trampolines
For fleas that grow like jumpin' beans,

Flitting to and fro.

Every day, old Lady LaMond,
Smitten with cats, was extra fond
Of our kitty cat, and cemented the bond,

With visits every day.

The cats were as greedy as she was barmy,
And one day, the keeper, whose name was Sammy,
Told me she fed the big cats salami,

Forced through the wire fence.

Things got tense when her folks couldn't find her –
They went to the pen, where an angle grinder,
Was lying by the gate, but with no sign of her,

Mouser or her mate.

We watched the cctv screen
As Sammy rewound and played the scene,
(The picture was grainy and sickly green),

And her folks began to pray.

A spray of sparks from the grinder blade,
Cut through the fence like sun through a glade,
Then she laced on her rollerblades,

And fixed the cats with reins.

They took the strain like a pair of huskies
And she made wide arcs, as though wearing jet-skis,
But whatever her quest, she seemed to freeze,

Like a dummy on a crash test.

She hit a ramp, went head over heels,
Somersaulting through ten cartwheels,
Then splashed in the pond while all the seals

Clapped and barked: R R...

*   *   *

She became the star of a WANTED poster
Showing a man drawin' a gun from a holster
While she was wrapped round his neck like a halter

Fastened on with spurs.

The square was packed with folks who read
Of the enormous bounty placed on her head –
If she was captured, alive or dead –

Five thousand pounds in cash!

Quite a stash to all concerned,
But with cats by now, I think we've learned;
The tables can very quickly be turned,

With the hunter being haunted.

Yet, undaunted by big cats at large,
A posse was gathered, and the man in charge
Was a bossy type by the name of 'Sarge',

Who spoke like a man with a grudge:

'I'm the judge, and I'm the jury,
So never fear, never worry,
I never fail to bring home the quarry,

Be it tiger, boar or quail.'

To prove he was hard, he wore a string-vest
In spite of the wind blowin' in from the west,
Though he seemed to grow a thicket or nest

Under each one of his armpits.

Belts of bullets crossed his chest,
And his bingo wings had tattooed crests
While his belly sagged under the hem of his vest

Like porridge skin on jelly.

His face was as smooth as an elephant's bum,
Ruddy and weathered by elements and rum,
But he winked at the women, chewed his gum,

And puffed on a big cigar.

A figure from the RSPCA
Spoke to the crowd in his PC way,
But his mellow tones could never sway

The posse with their guns.

'It wasn't their fault they escaped from the zoo;
They're noble beasts, majestic and true
To their nature, whatever your view,

There's no need to harm the creatures.'

One of the farmers finally laughed;
'If ya think I'm buyin' that crap you're daft,
You think I work and sweat and graft,

So they can eat my livestock?

When she goes a huntin' on private grounds,
The master takes care to lock up the hounds,
Since the night he heard bloodcurdlin' sounds,

Out there in the wood.

His favourite hounds; Rex and Max,
Had puncture wounds in the sides of their necks.
And it wasn't Count Drac; I saw the tracks:

Cat prints in the mud.'

'So listen '*Spud*', we're not for turnin',
Take your fancy words and stuff your sermon;
For there's only one thing to do with vermin',

Said Sarge, who'd heard enough.

'I'll take no guff from this silly mug,
C'mon boys, let's pull the plug;
I need to replace the old cat rug

Stretched out before the fireplace.'

They mounted a gun with a three-sixty-sweep,
And a powerful lamp on the roof of the jeep,
And the back was loaded with a monstrous heap

Of traps with shark-like jaws.

TRACKING THE BEASTS

The rumour mill worked just like a wireless,
So news from the hunt spread like a virus,
And this is what happened, more or less,

As far as I can glean:

Eyes of neon green, so bright,
Gave her away one fateful night,
When she froze in the frosty snare of light,

Beaming from the jeep.

Caught like a sheep at the end of the trail:
They fired their guns and a swarm of hail
Blattered from barrels as a dreadful wail,

Cursed the silent night.

By morning light, a trail of blood
Led their bloodhounds through the wood,
But all they found was a mewing brood

Of kittens in a tree stump.

They grabbed each 'clump' by the scruff of the neck;
Nine in all went into the sack,
Dragged along the mucky track

That leads down to the river.

The bag seemed to quiver as Sarge tied the knot,
And swung it overhead, like an ape, but got,
One hell of a gunk when a hail of grapeshot

Blasted through a tree trunk.

'Two can play at the macho game,
Now drop the bag, hang your heads in shame,
Then turn and go back the way you came',

Said Lady LaMond to the pack.

The posse backed up, then turned and ran,
Leaving old Sarge to carry the can
To that gun-totin' cat-doting harried old gran,

And so he began to plead:

'A cat will breed like a Russian doll,
Sure you'd never afford to feed them all;
It's best all round if we drown them all';

Said Sarge like a teddy bear.

'Harm a single hair on a single puss,'
She said, takin' aim with her blunderbuss,
'And you'll go home in a sarcophagus,

So what's it gonna be then?

A count of 10 is all I'll give,
Then we'll see how long you'll live
If you still refuse to follow my will, cos you've

Really lit my fuse.'

The bats in her belfry had all their screws loose;
There was no point in trying to call for a truce –
She cocked her gun and yelled '*Vamoose!*

You don't want to make me sore!

1,2,3,4,'
You could see the sweat begin to pour.
'5,6,7,8,'
Would 2 more seconds seal his fate?
'9,10,...'

And that was when
He turned to go and slowly pace,
Dragging his heels to save some face,
As I stepped out from behind a tree
With my catapult loaded, I raised the V
And stretched the rubber like bubble bum
While wedged in the V was his big fat bum.
Then just as Sarge felt the sting,
Lady LaMond let off a ring
Into the air like a starting gun
As Sarge took off on a marathon.

THE LEGEND

The trail of blood stopped dead in a clearing
But she'd disappeared in spite of her maiming,
Strange as the night of her first appearing,

Shivering with cold and fright.

Had she survived or had she deceased?
Fear on farms dramatically increased,
Till at last she became a mythical beast,

Stalking far and wide.

The countryside can never be policed
So now and again, when a sheep got fleeced,
Everyone knew who'd had the feast;

Though 'proof' is pretty slight.

Some night she'll be caterwaulin'
You'll be shakin' in your bed, your flesh'll be crawlin',
But that's how she'll communicate, when callin'

For her mate.

Her beginning and end is a mystery
And the rest as they say, is history,
But her legend lives on in her legacy:

The kittens with Lady LaMond.

THE EPI-MOG

'She was less of a pet, an' more of a pest,
But I miss her like hell', I confessed
To Lady La Mond, who happily "blessed"

Our home with one of the brood.

She yapped and mewed and looked so sad,
Shivering like she might well go mad,
Then clung to me like a velcro pad –

So I became her foster father.

Light as a feather, soft as lint,
Her innocent eyes gave no hint
Of sharpening fangs and nails of flint,

Growing all the while.

I was going to call the cat 'Maloney',
But La Mond said 'That's just a load of baloney.'
And pointing a finger that was long and boney

Said, 'The cat's called Ruby Roo!'

Her curiosity grew and grew
And through her we see the world anew;
Everything's fresh and magical too,

And spurs her on to high jinks.

She thinks the loo is a magic well
Cos when I flush a poo it casts a spell –
The waters gush, then rise and swell

Before it disappears.

Her ears stick up like horns on a bull
As the cistern gulps until it's full;
Then I give the chain another pull

And she peeps right over the rim.

For her each room is a wonderland
(Curiosity stretches like a rubberband)
But she'll tire then fall into slumberland

When she rolls up like a furball.

Her tongue's just like a sliver of soap,
And she licks her paws to give her more scope
Than I can get from 'soap-on-a-rope';

She's really got the knack –

She licks her back, she licks her tum,
She once took a spin in the washing drum,
She licks your face, she licks her bum;

And sometimes vice versa.

She runs up the curtains, an' she jumps on the chairs,
She spins 'round the table an' she bounds up the stairs,
She tears up my jeans an' she pees in my hair,

And shows us just what love means.

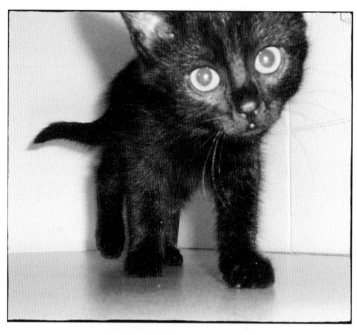